Foster Parenting Essentials

TOMMY STOREY

WESTBOW
PRESS®
A DIVISION OF THOMAS NELSON
& ZONDERVAN

Copyright © 2017 Tommy Storey.

All rights reserved. No part of this book may be used or reproduced by any means, graphic, electronic, or mechanical, including photocopying, recording, taping or by any information storage retrieval system without the written permission of the author except in the case of brief quotations embodied in critical articles and reviews.

The Living Bible copyright © 1971 by Tyndale House Foundation. Used by permission of Tyndale House Publishers Inc., Carol Stream, Illinois 60188. All rights reserved. The Living Bible, TLB, and the The Living Bible logo are registered trademarks of Tyndale House Publishers.

This book is a work of non-fiction. Unless otherwise noted, the author and the publisher make no explicit guarantees as to the accuracy of the information contained in this book and in some cases, names of people and places have been altered to protect their privacy.

WestBow Press books may be ordered through booksellers or by contacting:

WestBow Press
A Division of Thomas Nelson & Zondervan
1663 Liberty Drive
Bloomington, IN 47403
www.westbowpress.com
1 (866) 928-1240

Because of the dynamic nature of the Internet, any web addresses or links contained in this book may have changed since publication and may no longer be valid. The views expressed in this work are solely those of the author and do not necessarily reflect the views of the publisher, and the publisher hereby disclaims any responsibility for them.

Any people depicted in stock imagery provided by Thinkstock are models, and such images are being used for illustrative purposes only. Certain stock imagery © Thinkstock.

ISBN: 978-1-9736-0024-4 (sc)
ISBN: 978-1-9736-0025-1 (hc)
ISBN: 978-1-9736-0026-8 (e)

Library of Congress Control Number: 2017913139

Print information available on the last page.

WestBow Press rev. date: 8/25/2017

Dedication

To my beautiful wife Patricia
The true soul of our home

Now lovingly called
Mom by many

Thanks for always loving, supporting and believing

Contents

Introduction ix
Questionnaire xi

Chapter 1   Our Story 1
Chapter 2   Overview 9
Chapter 3   Characteristics of a Foster Parent 12
Chapter 4   Teaching Values 16
Chapter 5   New Child in Your Home 18
Chapter 6   Dynamics of the Home 21
Chapter 7   Be Specific with Children 23
Chapter 8   Fairness 24
Chapter 9   Social Skills 26
Chapter 10 Pre-Teaching 28
Chapter 11 Breath of Fresh Air 30
Chapter 12 Chores and Schedules and Keeping Busy 31
Chapter 13 Proper Emotions and Kindness 34
Chapter 14 Disrespect for Parents 35
Chapter 15 Children Face Many Pressures 37
Chapter 16 Morning Routine 39
Chapter 17 Professionalism 41
Chapter 18 Listen to Reports from Others 43
Chapter 19 Be Open to Criticism 45
Chapter 20 Make Memories 46

Chapter 21	Learning from Disagreement	49
Chapter 22	Keeping Your Sanity	50
Chapter 23	Sharing Disciplinary Duties	52
Chapter 24	Don't Be a Child's Peer	54
Chapter 25	Sexual Acting Out	55
Chapter 26	Avoiding Sexual Allegations	58
Chapter 27	Keeping Your Biological Family Together	60
Chapter 28	Working with Families	63
Chapter 29	Cultural Awareness	67
Chapter 30	Splitting	69
Chapter 31	Learning to Let Go	70
Chapter 32	Exaggerated Illness	72
Chapter 33	Confrontation, Unpleasant but Important	73
Chapter 34	Power Struggles	81
Chapter 35	Physical Restraint	83
Chapter 36	Faith and Worship	88
Chapter 37	Conclusion	90

Introduction

My wife and I have been in direct childcare longer than anyone we know. Over the years we have heard many comments from our families and perfect strangers concerning our roles as foster parents. The comments range from, "You're kidding!" to, "You must be crazy!" The one we have heard most often is, "You and your wife must be wonderful people to do what you do. I could never do that. I don't know how you do it!" My standard reply is an emphatic, "I don't know how we do it either!"

I pondered this for a long time before it dawned on me that very few people have any idea what our lives are like, much less how we do it. This includes caseworkers, case managers, other foster parents, supervisors, administrators, and even our own families.

Many children are in care across our nation. If few people know how we do it, then who is training the caregivers and with what? I have come to realize there is little practical information in print about surviving and performing our duties as caregivers. There are thousands of therapeutic and psychological books. There is little written about surviving the day-to-day battle and struggle of raising emotionally damaged children while maintaining your sanity, keeping everyone safe, and teaching positive values.

This is why I felt compelled to write the words that follow. Everything here is written simply and is drawn from experience coupled with what I feel are useful strategies to deal with problems along with other topics of interest to caregivers of children. My wife and I have many positive and pleasant memories; however, most questions asked of us concern problems and their solutions. This book is mostly written from that angle. I wish someone had furnished this information to us years ago.

I never dreamed of or wanted to write a book, but I feel we are sometimes chosen to do things we had not planned on doing, as is the case in our professions as well. God sometimes places things in our hearts without asking us for our opinions.

Every day for my wife and me is a struggle, just as it is for everyone else in life, regardless of where you are. We do not have all the answers and never will. Hopefully others can learn from our experiences and develop helpful insights from our successes, failures, and often humbling and embarrassing memories. This is our story plus short lessons from experience.

If these words can help one caregiver cope and then help a child, my time writing was well spent.

Questionnaire

Please answer the following questions with *yes* or *no*; an explanation will follow:

1. Have you ever had a child in your care change from street clothing into a bathing suit by your picnic table at Hurricane Harbor in front of several thousand people without your noticing?

2. Have you ever gone to the cashier at a restaurant to pay for your family's meal and had a child in your care bring you several dollar bills in cash and then go on and on about how you had forgotten your money by your plate on the table?

3. Have you ever realized at a football game that you are the only parent with children of three different races asking you for money and calling you Dad?

4. Have you ever had a child urinate on your dining chair after you left the room?

5. Have you ever had a child go to school and convince her class and teacher that her foster parents would not be giving her any Christmas presents and then get everyone in the class to pitch in to buy her gifts?

6. Have you ever proudly been the father of the first black cheerleader in an all-white high school?

7. Have you ever realized that when you let your children out of your van at school, parents look at you as they would at the clown driving the car in the parade that stops and fourteen people get out? The looks on their faces say, "How did they do that?"

8. Have you ever gone to school to pick up a child for a doctor's visit and found yourself giving a physical description of the child to the school secretary because you can't remember the child's name?

9. Have you ever had the privilege of eating for free at Taco Bell because the cashier thought you were a bus driver, and bus drivers eat for free? It's their policy!

10. Have you ever come to the realization that among your friends in your age group, you are the only one who can translate gang signs and symbols into English?

If you answered yes to any of these questions, you are either a foster parent or are possibly foster parent material. I am the only person I know who can answer yes to *all* of them.

1

Our Story

We have truly been blessed. Sometimes I forget, but it is true. My wife, children, and I now live in the home I was raised in on a small Texas ranch, although from my perspective, it has had renovations and expansions that rival the building of the great pyramids of Egypt. This ranch has been in my family since the 1800s, but nothing like what we do has ever occurred here before. I literally built and renovated this home day and night for two and a half years while operating a group home and working another career. How my wife and I remained together during all of this is almost unimaginable. Tricia tells our friends we stayed together because we were both too tired to do anything else. There is probably at least a little truth in that theory. Besides operating a foster home, I also operate an auction business—acquired from my father—that has been in business for almost sixty years.

My wife and I were raised in Christian homes that were very much isolated from most of the abuses in the world. We didn't know what foster care was. No one could have been less prepared to raise foster children than we were; however, I know God brought us to this place, training us along the way. I must admit, though, that he kept what he was doing completely to himself until it was too late for us to back out.

My wife and I have children by birth and adoption in addition to grandchildren. All have been a blessing. Most everything that I can remember of my early adult years I am ashamed to tell, and hopefully God will keep quiet about it as well.

At the age of thirty-one, without warning to anyone, I informed my father and my wife that I would go to college to get my teaching degree. My wife and I had three children at the time. My father said, and I repeat, "That is impossible." My wife was younger than I was and was not aware that she was soon to become my superior. She said okay because she didn't know what else to say. We endured some hard times during college, but I graduated two years and nine months later with a teaching degree in education and not an extra credit to spare. Looking back on it now, I know it was God's will because, as my father had said, it was impossible! But it happened! This would open many doors for us later.

During my first year of teaching, I began to learn humility and that I was not entirely in charge of my future. This is quite opposite from the message in many self-help books. Someone else was at the steering wheel.

My wife's best friend from high school and her husband were employed at a well-respected therapeutic residential treatment center for children. They had been there for a few years and had tried to recruit us to come to work during my college career. After my first year of teaching, we decided to accept the offer. The main selling points were that we could work together, room and board were provided in a very nice home, and food and transportation were furnished. All that would be required was to care for eight boys, ranging from six to eighteen years old. Easy! Right?

Our friends were supervisors at the ranch, and when a couple resigned, our friends were required to move into that home until suitable replacements could be found. Two things made us suspicious that the job might be more difficult than it seemed. The first was that our friends telephoned us almost daily to make sure of when we would be arriving. Second, upon our arrival at the very large and imposing home, our friends seemed extremely relieved. They and the boys quickly unloaded our truck. Our friends then drove off into the night after explaining that they would be by the next day to fill us in. Looking back, I don't know why we didn't drive off ourselves.

The training was very thorough, and we were under constant scrutiny. The teaching method used a point system for behavior modification. This point system was individualized for each child, and basically the number of points each boy acquired daily would determine his privileges for the next. Each child was required to have a certain number of signed interactions on a card for each day. This is a simplistic description of a confrontational system that, when taught correctly, would increase positive behaviors and decrease negative behaviors. We learned to write treatment plans, manage a large household smoothly, and reward and confront both positive and negative behaviors.

It was over six months before we had time to unpack our boxes from the move. To be honest, if we had not had children depending on us, or if we'd had another job waiting on us, we would have quit.

It was a tough job. We were up early, busy until late at night, and tired all the time. At first, we seemed unable to get the children to do anything without a tremendous amount of confrontation and stress. The other parents at the ranch told us often that after six months things would become easier. Six months seemed like an eternity, but in the seventh month, things did become easier. We were catching on.

There were many amenities at the ranch, such as a swimming pool, tickets to baseball games, and other activities. Our family finally settled in. After a year and a half, another son was born. During my wife's pregnancy, I sometimes was forced by necessity to care for our children and the eight boys in our care single-handedly. That was a tough time for me personally. I learned a lot about myself and what was required of a sole caregiver.

Soon after our son was born, we moved into a girls' home to learn different lessons. We thought we had gone to heaven. The girls were much more social and less aggressive. We now dealt with more emotional baggage and less physical aggression. Sometimes we could even leave them unattended for short periods without worrying about the physical aggression we had become used to in the boys' home. It was a welcome change.

Almost everything we know about behavior modification and confrontation was learned in those homes. It was not always fun, but we are eternally grateful for the training we received.

After three years, my wife became a supervisor, and I became a supervisor for the local mental health department. She supervised group homes on the ranch. I supervised group homes, staff, and clients with mental disabilities. I was also in charge of taking care of behavioral problems and training staff. My wife and I learned many new things during this period. Instead of saying, "I can't believe they did that," I began using the phrase, "Well, I've never seen that before."

We moved back to our hometown after four years so that I might take a position as a vocational teacher at a juvenile correctional facility. We found that our friends who had recruited us originally were now in charge of a newly formed foster care program at the largest therapeutic center for children in that area. They soon asked us to open the first therapeutic group home in our community. That soon became a reality. At that time, it was uncharted territory for everyone involved, although now there are many such homes.

My wife and I are most likely the busiest people I have ever met. At one time we had twelve foster children in our home. If you knew me personally, you would probably think I appeared laid-back and never in a big hurry. I guess it is my slow Texas upbringing. What people don't realize is that I sometimes may seem slow because I am often exhausted, as is my wife, from the many parts of our daily lives that most people don't know about. When I go to bed, I am most likely at least two hours late, and when I arrive at work, I have already been busy for two hours. Every day is usually the same. It takes all day—and then some—for both of us to get the most important things done. Everything else that occurs is just icing on the cake.

On a related note, we never oversleep more than a few minutes in the mornings. If we do, I will wake up as if from a bad nightmare. You will understand completely if you have ever tried to get almost a dozen teenage girls dressed and out the door for school in a big hurry, followed by writing an "I'm sorry _____ is tardy" note for each child. We just cannot be late waking up. If we are, the planet will actually stop rotating.

Back to the "busy" thing: My wife is not a morning person. I'm not either, but early in our career I must have drawn the short straw—although I don't recall drawing. My job is usually to get everyone in the home up and ready for school before coming back home and changing vehicles to go to work at my business. My wife's day usually begins at that time. She has a Day Runner that she uses to keep up with appointments and such. Most days are completely filled for her, until the kids come home from school with doctor and dentist appointments, school visits, psychologist appointments, treatment plannings and staffings, grocery shopping, progress note writing, medication logs, appointments to talk to caseworkers, etc. During all of these activities, she will often receive a phone call from a child at school requesting to come home because of some phantom illness. This attempt usually fails because we have a standing policy in our home that you must be throwing up to get a home pass; however, after that rule took effect, we later added "with fever" as a requirement because developing a fever is much harder to learn to do on cue. Many children apparently don't like school very much.

Our lives are much different from those of our parents. I believe my wife's cell phone number is on the principal's speed dial. Is that crazy or what? I don't even think my parents knew who my principal was when I was a child.

Most of our children will arrive home by school bus at about four o'clock. Our home is approximately two hundred yards from the highway bus stop. I remember being behind the bus once when it stopped at the end of our lane and I watched our children get off. I swear some of them were going in the front door of my home before the last child had gotten off the bus. Traffic appeared to have been backed up for miles. Okay, this is an exaggeration. It only seemed like miles, but I did consider driving past my lane so that the people behind me wouldn't think I lived there. Also, one of my friends once commented that he really hated being behind the school bus when it stopped at our house.

My wife is usually the person at home to greet the children after school. Sometimes I begin a personal bus route about this time. I am a glorified and underpaid taxi driver. We usually have children in many activities, and because all of their instructors are totally committed to being the best, they usually have many after-school practices.

I can't find it in the school handbook, but I believe it is school policy for all practices to be as inconvenient to the parents as possible. One child will practice until five minutes after the school bus leaves school. Another will be finished with practice at four o'clock and will need to be picked up immediately in order to be back at school at eight o'clock for a different practice session. Two more children will probably be finished at five thirty, and another should be getting off work thirty minutes later. Just as I get settled into my recliner, I will sometimes receive a phone call informing me that the last child will be arriving at school in fifteen minutes from a basketball game. The child will need to be picked up immediately so as not to inconvenience the coaches. I had a recorder installed on my satellite dish, and it is one of my favorite personal possessions.

I once made nine trips to school in the same day. During one afternoon last week, I drove 180 miles and was never more than eight miles away from my home at any one time. This is absolutely true!

During all of this, my wife and I cook a meal and dine. All the children take baths, finish homework, complete chores, and ask to use the telephone three times each. We have a girls' home! Between eight and nine o'clock my wife will usually retire to our bedroom for some quiet time. I understand why, and she deserves it.

For the first fifteen years we were in this field we never slept with our bedroom door shut, and we never took a Sunday afternoon nap at the same time. Someone needed to be able to monitor the house in order for all to be safe and coexist in peace. I have recently learned that I can occasionally take a nap on a Sunday afternoon at the same time as my wife with few misadventures. I first talk to the girls and tell them where I am going. These are the exact words I use before leaving them: "Girls, I am going to take a nap. Be quiet, and don't argue or fight. Don't come get me unless you see blood or the house is on fire." Luckily, they seldom wake me.

This account of a day in our life may seem humorous, but it is true. I tell all of this for a reason. Anyone wanting to do what we do needs to know the facts. This is a hard 24/7 job that is very tiring and totally consuming. What I didn't mention above is that during all of this activity, we are dealing with children who have a powder keg of emotions that can explode at any time. We are teaching them proper manners and behaviors while settling quarrels. We will often find ourselves empathizing with a child over a problem or the child's personal tragedies and previous abuse. We are constantly teaching positive behaviors and confronting negative behaviors. We do this from the time we wake up until bedtime. It never ends. If it does, our home is out of control in a heartbeat. Remember, teaching must never end. All inappropriate behaviors must be addressed as they happen, not when convenient. This is how children are helped to get better and become prepared for later in life. Add a little love and tenderness to the teaching, and it becomes even more successful.

2

Overview

In 2015, in Texas, there were 290,471 allegations of child abuse or neglect; 66,721 confirmed abuse or neglect cases; 17,151 children removed from their homes; and 27,895 children in child protective custody at year's end. These are statistics for only one state. Many thousands more across the nation are also in care.

In the past, most children in the care of the state were housed in large group settings with shift workers as caregivers. Some were residential treatment centers; others were assessment centers.

The emphasis now is to try to place the majority of children into private foster homes in communities near where the child may have lived before. Some of these homes have single parents, and some have married couples, but all are operated in as close to a normal home environment as possible. This is the goal. If children are raised in private foster homes, it is believed by experts that they may more easily transition back into society upon reaching adulthood.

Many willing and able parents are needed, but few are trained, and many feel they are not capable.

These pages will most likely be of interest to you only if you now work with children in the foster care system or may be considering joining this profession and ministry in the future. Trust me. It is a ministry.

In the following, I am going to pass on to you much of what I have learned—mostly practical, teachable things—in order to prepare you to be successful. My wife and I do not have all answers to all situations and still have much more to learn. What I can do is share some basic strategies, experiences, and instructions that have worked for us or for others we know. I will also share many things to avoid. You will need to consider your personality and strengths in light of what I share for it to be practical and help you succeed. All children are different, but many share common behaviors and problems. All caregivers are different, and each will bring to the table different strengths and weaknesses, along with common basic emotions. All situations will be different because of our differences and uniqueness, but in many situations, you will find commonalities.

What has worked for us could possibly work for you or possibly stop a negative situation from developing.

The children in our country who need help have many problems and abuse issues never before seen in this magnitude in our society. Most children in care come from broken homes with exposure to drug and alcohol abuse. Many have been abused to a degree that is unimaginable. My wife and I have cared for children with stories that would make the strongest among us shed tears. I refuse to repeat much of what I have seen or witnessed because of the terrible nature of the abuse. Some children have not suffered as severely, but all have been neglected. All have abandonment issues and are lonely, scared, and desperate.

Those of you who have a basic understanding of elementary psychology will know that children are most often products of their childhood environments. Their personalities are shaped at an early age. If left in negative environments, they will become what they came from. If their parents were neglectful, they will be. If their parents lied and cursed, they will lie and curse. If they have suffered abuse sexually or physically, then they will have tendencies to abuse others in the same ways.

As a person who takes one of these children into your home, you must be willing to address negative and antisocial behaviors and habits learned from birth. There will be many and will vary from child to child depending on age, personality, and degree of abuse.

Most children can be helped. Many will recover completely with the right teaching, but it is not an easy task and requires special dedicated people and the resources of many others.

3
Characteristics of a Foster Parent

I have found, and this is my personal opinion only, that there are basically four types of foster parents or caregivers.

The first type of person could be in the profession because of circumstances. People of this type may not feel this is their place in life, but they need to fill in for someone else until a later time. These are usually very good people and may often be related to the children, such as grandparents, uncles, or aunts. They do not want to make a career of this.

The second type of person I see interested in this ministry is what I call the "bleeding hearts" of the world. There are many. Most people of this type believe that love alone will fix most everyone and everything. They feel that all the child's former abuse can be corrected if a foster parent has a loving heart. They are correct in the respect that love is needed; however, much more is required than love. Most of these people expect an outpouring of gratitude from the child they are caring for. This is a selfish motivation for becoming a foster parent, although it is not readily apparent to outsiders. People of this type will not last long as foster parents because many children are incapable of expressing or feeling gratitude. It may be delayed for a long time, or it may never be expressed. These people will often soon become disenchanted and move on. To succeed as a foster parent, you must have the inner strength to continue because it is right and needs to be done and not because you are expecting thanks from the children.

Another type of person attracted to this industry will often see an opportunity to make money and will use this as their motivation. These people are often uncaring individuals who have the ability to appear very caring at first glance. They are simply looking for an easy dollar and believe this is it. They are often unable and unwilling to provide what is needed to help children. They will usually do what is easiest for themselves without considering the child's welfare. We have too many of these individuals in our profession now, and they give all of us a bad reputation because of their trademark actions. Believe me: if you are becoming a foster parent for the money, there are much easier ways to earn income that will not deny a child the opportunity to live with a nurturing and committed family.

Finally, this hopefully brings me to you, the type of person I feel is needed for our profession. There are many out there who are unaware of their calling or abilities—good people with high morals, solid values, and loving hearts. I feel that some will have it in their hearts to pursue this without a lot of coaxing. It will just seem right. People of this type just need patience, understanding, and stubbornness for the right reasons. Sometimes this profession will allow someone with small children of his or her own to care for a foster child and not have to work outside the home. Foster parents will most likely be compensated financially; that is fine if their hearts are where they should be, which is the case for this type. The Bible teaches us to compensate ministers and teachers, and as I said, foster parents are a type of minister.

If the above describes you, great, but you need to do a lot of soul searching and make sure you are totally committed before you begin. It can be devastating to a child in care to discover their foster parents are quitting and they are going to be sent to a new family. Children are like adults in that they can only deal with a limited amount of rejection.

As a caregiver, you will need to be fair to a fault and without prejudices.

You will need to have the ability to start each day fresh without grudges or hurt feelings from the previous day.

You will need to be a good finder. By that I mean you must have the ability to find the good qualities in others. The Bible says, "Seek and ye shall find." No truer words have ever been written. They are especially true when working with troubled children.

You must be truthful always. The children we care for have been deceived all their lives. Always tell the truth to a child and keep your promises. It will help build a child's trust in you, and it is the cornerstone of any good relationship. For a home to run smoothly, all children must know in their hearts that you are telling the truth in all matters. This concerns both pleasant and unpleasant truths.

You must be firm in your expectations and empathetic while maintaining focus on the child's welfare.

There is no substitute for good judgment coupled with common sense. Most problems or educational deficiencies can be overcome with these qualities.

You must be stubborn to a fault but in a professional manner. By this I mean that when disciplining or supporting a child, you must remain with the task as long as it takes to finish it.

You must have a sense of humor. When you are stressed the most, you must be able to step back and find the humor in the moment or the day's events. There is usually a lot of humor if you can look at things from an outsider's point of view.

You need to be a basically happy person. I have found that most people are about as happy as they decide to be, and that applies here to the greatest degree. Happiness and thankfulness are contagious.

I know this list seems long, and it is. Very few people possess all of these qualities at all times, but many possess most of these qualities, and the others can be learned. This profession can be quite tiring and stressful. I have seen the marriages of many good people in the childcare field come apart and end in divorce. If your marriage is shaky, stay away until it improves. But if you feel this is your calling, most things can be learned or improved with training and work. You will learn with time, with help from others, and with guidance from above.

My wife and I knew little when we began. We have survived and become better with the help of others and the grace of God. If we can, anyone can!

Possibly that someone is you!

4

Teaching Values

When a child is placed into your home, he or she will need to learn proper values. Your home needs to have rules and expectations, and all need to know them. Inappropriate language or actions should never be tolerated. Our children are never allowed to possess suggestive or obscene magazines, books, clothing, posters, or music that we find objectionable. Some children will tell you that it is their right to listen to any music or watch any television program they desire. It isn't. They must live by your morals, which I hope are high. We put all CDs or other things we find objectionable into a locked closet until the owner leaves our home.

Only a poor parent would allow a desperate child to listen to music with suicidal, satanic, or obscene lyrics. Nothing good can come from it.

Be firm and consistent. Make sure all comply.

The best teaching comes from good role modeling. Don't be doing one thing and telling your children to do something else—including cursing, gossiping, belittling others, procrastinating, avoiding responsibility for your own actions, etc. Look at what you do in front of the kids objectively, and see if you're consistent. The children in your home will notice if you aren't. Actions speak louder than words. Never be afraid to apologize when you make a mistake. Everyone makes mistakes from time to time, and apologizing is another example of good role modeling. Say thank you to a child when he or she does something for you or another peer. It is important for children to hear and learn about gratitude through a parent's words and role modeling. Praise as many positive things concerning a child's behavior as possible. This will increase the child's self-worth and will soften the sting from the negative interactions that are sometimes required. In general, speak positive words to and about the children in your care. Words can often become self-fulfilling prophecies. There are many passages in the Bible concerning this. When we are upset or aggravated, being positive is sometimes hard to do, but it is well worth the effort.

5

New Child in Your Home

When a child new to your home arrives, it can be a stressful time for both the child and caregiver. Do not be overly compliant or give special treatment, as this can cause many problems later. After the newness wears off, the child will continue to expect the same special treatment he or she received when first moving in. This is an unsustainable situation.

When a child moves into your home, you should welcome the child warmly, show him or her around, and explain the rules and expectations. You need to probably ask a few polite questions, but don't ask too many. Just treat the child as you would any of the other children. If you have a child in your home whom you trust and who has lived with you for a good while, let him or her make the child feel at home and help the new child settle in.

Most children will not act as they normally do when they first move in. This is often called the "honeymoon period." It may last a few days or a very long time. During this period, the child is sizing you up and trying to learn about you. When he or she begins to feel comfortable, the honeymoon is over.

When the honeymoon is over, the child will usually begin to act out to some degree. The most violent outbursts or tantrums will often occur at this time. The child will test your limits concerning his or her every action and desire. This is the time for consistency. During this period of time, your most important parent-to-child interactions will occur. You are paving the road ahead in your relationship. Be your best in every way you can. Confront and address all behaviors, both good and bad. Be fair, and set your limits. What happens next is often predestined during this difficult period.

We have been raising other people's children for a very long time, so I am speaking from experience.

During this initial transition of a child into your home, there will be an inevitable blowup after the child is confronted concerning a negative behavior. During the parent-child interaction, the child will often verbalize such statements as, "Why don't you just get rid of me then?" This is just a test. Don't buy into it. Many parents respond negatively, which leads to a long, unproductive discussion. In this interaction the child is drawing upon past failures in relationships and abandonment issues. It is sad but not for discussion at this time. The child is hoping you will feel sorry for him or her and therefore forget about the negative behavior, thus getting you off task. Kids do not like to be confronted. Rather than make a change, they would rather discuss a therapy issue. It is just a ploy to change the subject. In this situation we usually say, "We are not getting rid of anyone. That isn't even open for discussion. What we are going to do, though, is deal with the problem we are having now." Leave it at that. The child can discuss it later with his or her therapist or with you at a neutral time.

Often during an interaction concerning a negative issue the child will demand to call his or her caseworker. The child is able to talk to his or her caseworker, but we insist it is after tempers have cooled and problems resolved. If you allow a child to call his or her caseworker every time there is a disagreement, you and the caseworker both will soon be worn out over useless chatter. You are the parents, and you are in charge. When the child has cooled down, you may ask if he or she would like to call; most of the time they will decline because it was only another attempt to keep from dealing with the issue. Follow your agency's guidelines, of course.

Some children will test you in another way. They will try to get you to defend yourself and your house rules. They will say things like, "My last placement was much better," or "I sure was close to my last foster mom." This is another test. They are just testing limits. If you are insecure or unsure of yourself, it will work. If it does, the child will have the ability to hurt you anytime, and he or she will know it. That is a real power. We just act nonchalant about such comments and say things like, "I'm sorry, but this is the way we do it here," or "It's a shame you had to leave, isn't it?" Then we just act as if we never had the discussion. Use your best poker face. If you do, the child will learn this strategy will not work and will soon cease trying it.

By avoiding the normal urge to defend yourself or the rules of your home, you are learning and growing into the role of a successful caregiver.

6

Dynamics of the Home

Each home has a different air or feel. It is almost like a living being or entity. It is as individual as a fingerprint. It is the sum and expression of all the inhabitants. This is relevant to working with children.

One child can leave your home, and the feel of the home will change. All the children in the home will sometimes behave differently. If a new child moves in, then the same will often happen.

This is why: As parents, you will never be aware of everything that is happening in your home and how some children are interacting out of your presence. Even parents with much experience never know everything. If you think you do, you are naive. The higher-functioning children will sometimes act much differently away from you than when you are watching. Remember when you were a child? I doubt you always acted the same around your parents as you did when with your friends. It is the same in your home.

The lower-functioning or smaller children will most likely act much the same at all times because of less-developed social skills.

If there is more than one child in your home, then you can be certain there is always a struggle to establish a pecking order. This is natural. This explains why when your home's makeup or occupants change, there will often be a lot of behavioral outbursts and arguments. This will occur even with the children who have been in your care for years. After a while, the atmosphere will usually settle, but be prepared for the initial upheaval in your home.

7

Be Specific with Children

Be specific to a fault when telling a child what you expect. Children can have the ability to confuse what you think are simple instructions. My wife and I once had a girl in our home who was to attend the senior prom. My wife instructed her to be home by twelve o'clock. Needless to say, we were concerned when she was not home by midnight as expected. She returned home at twelve o'clock noon on the following day, thinking she was right on time.

The art of being specific has saved us from many problems and has many daily applications with children. We have learned to not assume anything when it comes to a child understanding what you expect from him or her.

A good way to make sure that children understand your expectations or instructions is to ask them to repeat your words back to you. Often you will discover the child never heard you to begin with.

8

Fairness

If you were to conduct a survey of people today and ask them if they are fair, I would venture to say that almost 100 percent would say yes. If you were to ask the people who know them, I would bet the percentage would be much smaller. How is it that we can view ourselves so differently from others? I just assume it is just a part of the human condition.

Fairness in all areas when dealing with children is perhaps the fastest way to win their hearts and develop a relationship. When I say *fairness*, I am really just meaning doing what is right.

If you have more than one child in your home, then you will most likely have one you instinctively like or prefer over another child. It could be because of the child's physical nature, personality, wit, or any other characteristic. It is only natural to sometimes talk to that child more or perhaps react differently to him or her than you would one of the other children.

To be a good caregiver you need to understand this and guard against it. Learn your own tendencies and treat all alike. All children deserve to be treated as equals. Our country is founded on this belief. Many children have poor self-esteem and have been beaten down by society. They have suffered through many unfair events. Make sure that you go out of your way to treat all alike so that everyone's self-esteem will increase and not just the self-esteem of your favorite one.

Make sure that when you give a consequence or reward it is fair and equal to the circumstance. Do not overreact or underreact to a situation because of personal bias.

If you can remain fair and impartial to all, then the children will pick up on this quickly, and many doors of opportunity involving your relationships with them may be opened.

We have noticed that if you are a fair person, most children will become loyal to you over time. At times they may curse at you or cause a problem for you, but if someone else does, they will come to your defense. If a child should make a false allegation against you, then it is almost a sure bet that the rest of the home will defend you. This happens because they have developed a sense of fairness from your role modeling.

People will forget what you said.

People will forget what you did.

People never forget how you made them feel.

—Unknown

9

Social Skills

Most abused or neglected children come into care with poor social skills. The term "raised by wolves" has a lot of meaning to my wife and me.

Most children will almost have to start from zero as far as social skills go. Manners must be taught. Appropriate dress must be taught. The ability to interact with others and act correctly in a public setting will be required teaching on a daily basis.

Remember, if a child was raised in an inappropriate environment for ten years, then it would follow that you would not be able to correct all problems in six months or even a year. It is not possible. Only God performs miracles.

Children raised in neglectful environments often have little control over their emotions. They are referred to as "emotionally disturbed" for good reason. Some will laugh when they should cry, and others will curse when they should respond with a simple yes. Children will taunt others when they should show sympathy or concern. Many children will show no emotion. I once witnessed a sixteen year old looking at the faces of her peers to see their expressions. Her face was blank, and she quite literally was unable to come up with the correct emotional response from within.

Children are often unable to say "thank you" because they are incapable of feeling gratitude. This is why in this line of work you will often get few of the warm fuzzy feelings you thought you would get after helping a child. Gratitude from some children will come later and sometimes never at all.

Working with emotionally disturbed children is busy and often not gratifying at the time. As the old saying goes, "When you are up to your waist in a swamp full of alligators, it is hard to remember the objective was to drain the swamp." Your patience, perseverance, and God will take care of the alligators. Focus on the swamp.

If you can teach proper social skills on a consistent basis, then you can often change a child's future to a degree hard to imagine. Social skills are often an important deciding factor between success and failure in life. We have seen many miracles come later, and sometimes long after a child has left our home, because of having learned proper social skills.

10

Pre-Teaching

Pre-teaching is an easily learned tool that can save you trouble and time and prevent many problems. Pre-teaching means that as a parent you will try to anticipate a potential problem or situation before it occurs and discuss with your children the proper actions they should take when the problem or situation arises. Discuss with the child your exact expectations concerning the potential problem.

A good example might be if you are about to attend a football game. Before you get out of the vehicle, you might instruct your children to be sure to stay in the fenced area, do not go under the bleachers, and do not go out into the parking lot. This clarifies what you expect and makes it more likely that they will follow your rules. It also lets them know what you are going to be watching for. Pre-teaching will often prevent negative situations from occurring when they most likely would have if not for the warning.

Another aspect of pre-teaching is that is lets your children learn that you are going to hold them accountable for their actions. That knowledge is always needed. All successful adults have been taught at a young age to be accountable for their actions. This is done by thinking before acting and weighing the benefits against the consequences. By pre-teaching you are helping the child learn to think before acting. Over time, this can slow down a child's impulsive nature if used correctly and often.

Also, if they do a good job of following your expectations, express that you are proud of them.

11

Breath of Fresh Air

After you have been a caregiver for a period of time, you sometimes become jaded by all the terrible things you have heard, and you feel sad because of the lost innocence of the children you care for. Few things are sadder than the lost innocence of a small child. On the other hand, every once in a while God will send a breath of fresh air.

My wife often tells this story of a young girl of about ten years old who was in our care. At that time we had several girls in our home. Some were older and much less innocent. While riding in the van, the girls were discussing boys, as girls often do. Out of the blue, this ten-year-old girl said, "I hate boys!" This was age appropriate, but my wife decided to ask her why. Everyone's jaw dropped when she said, "All they want is one thing!" Everyone in the van had one thought until the girl said, "Yeah, all they want is your candy!" Everyone laughed. Apparently she was referring to a lost Christmas candy episode from her past. Some children in your care may still have some innocence left.

12

Chores and Schedules and Keeping Busy

Every child in our home has a chore. We have a chore list posted on the refrigerator. It changes weekly. One week a chore might be to set and clear before meals, another week it might be dishes, etc. We try to pass the chores around evenly. Each child receives an allowance, which is compensation for doing his or her chore. Chores are usually completed by eight o'clock at night.

We expect all children in our care to make their beds and clean their rooms each morning. They also wash their own clothes weekly.

Some foster parents do these things themselves for the children, but unless you have small children, I believe each child should do as we do in our home.

The reason for the chores is that all children should learn how to take care of themselves and not be taken care of. They will be all alone in the world in a short time and will need these skills to survive.

There are several reasons that rooms are clean and picked up and beds are made each morning. Most of our children have low self-esteem and sometimes feel powerless over their own lives. If they have clean rooms, then that is something they can control and can feel good about. It isn't a lot, but it does help build self-esteem quicker than some would think. It helps make their lives seem less chaotic, and it helps them take pride in our home and their home. Some of the poorest organizers and worst slobs I have known have become almost neat freaks after a while. Good things, when done daily, become good habits and make for an easier life. These simple practices can often transfer to other areas later in life.

If you feel you need to explain to the kids why their rooms need to be clean, tell them, "People come to our home a lot, and your room represents you. We want them to see you in a good way. It's just like combing your hair in the morning."

Inspect what you expect. You should always spot-check chores and rooms. If you don't, they will be done poorly, and the wrong lesson will be learned. We try to teach everyone to do a good job always. We just expect it. Sometimes consequences will have to be issued if a child will not comply, and often a positive reward is given to those who do as asked.

At times you may have a problem with some of the children finishing their chores correctly and on time. There are two different ways to handle the situation other than one-on-one with negative consequences being delivered.

We have been known to tell everyone who did as expected to get in the van, and my wife might then take them out for a milkshake. At other times it is more effective to get the children in your home to police it themselves. You may do this by issuing group consequences until all comply. An example might be to say there will be no television allowed on a given night because everyone's rooms were not clean that morning. Never underestimate the ability of children to keep others in line. This tactic is used in every athletic program I know of. Sometimes the entire basketball team will have to run laps or something else because of one person's actions. In the real world, often a whole business will suffer because of the actions of one or two.

As a caregiver of several children, you must learn to keep them busy. Plan daily activities in the summer that use energy and keep them occupied. Go places, even if it is just to the city park. Municipal pools are great places to visit. Libraries are good once-a-week visits that also give them something constructive to do in their free time. Keep them busy, or they will keep you busy!

Have a definite schedule, and stick to it as much as possible. Dysfunctional children behave much better if they know what to expect. They need structure and want it even though they may say differently. Try to keep to a definite bedtime unless there are special situations or activities. I expect my children to start settling down and getting quiet about an hour before bedtime. This helps get them to bed without problems. Be sure to exclude physical activities before bedtime, as some children have a very hard time turning it off to go to bed.

We never allow our children to roughhouse indoors and seldom outside. If they do, it will often lead to fights and hurt feelings. Emotionally disturbed children have a hard time getting themselves under control after physical exertion.

13

Proper Emotions and Kindness

Learn how to be unemotional in a crisis and focused on your task. Just as importantly, learn how to convey genuine sympathetic emotions when justified. Kids need to see both sides of your personality in order to find a balance in their own actions and lives.

Children have learned to respond negatively to situations from role models in their early lives. Try to be the person who models the correct emotional response at the correct time. How you handle yourself nonverbally when you're sad or tired will often be remembered long after your words are forgotten. Part of the human condition is to be emotional. Make sure you display the right ones yourself at the correct times.

Of all the emotions and qualities that need to be taught, kindness and empathy are probably the most important and can be taught only by example. Go out of your way to show this every day to everyone. Kindness is one thing that can be given away daily without the storeroom becoming empty.

14

Disrespect for Parents

Before my wife and I became foster parents, we had been cursed at very few times. No one likes being cursed at, so most of us learn how to avoid it. After we became foster parents, we soon learned that avoiding this was often impossible in our new line of work. This was a tough and totally unexpected lesson.

Emotionally disturbed children have often learned to disrespect adults at an early age. They often have zero inhibitions about cursing at an adult authority figure. This can be an excellent indication that a child is emotionally disturbed. Most children raised in a positive, nurturing environment will automatically know this behavior is wrong and unacceptable. They will just not do it.

If you are a caregiver in a therapeutic environment, you will be cursed at and yelled at. This negative behavior was learned early, and you are simply the next person in line.

You must control your anger even though you may want to lash back at the child. You must control your anger.

A successful caregiver will remain calm and detached from his or her negative feelings during a verbal assault. He or she will also remain focused on the issue at hand and not be distracted by the verbal barrage. It is unacceptable and unproductive to do anything less.

If you have failed at this in the past, then cheer up and move on. Everyone will fall prey to this mistake at some time. It's normal. With experience and practice, you will soon master the skills needed to avoid this, and other important skills will begin to fall into place also.

Remember, if the child doesn't get the response expected from you after a verbal attack, he or she will most likely display such negative behaviors less frequently toward you and hopefully toward others as well.

Modeling proper anger control is one of the best lessons you will teach. Proper anger control is essential for a child to learn to be successful.

15

Children Face Many Pressures

All children in modern society face temptations, negative situations, and propaganda that is almost unimaginable. Modern-day children face more pressures in a few days than I did in my entire childhood.

Our children are bombarded daily with high-tech negative pressures. If a child desired, he or she could access almost anything from the Internet, video store, music store, video gaming room, or even a local superstore. These accessible items range from pornography to the unimaginable, and most are detrimental to a positive childhood. You will never be able to shelter a child from everything, because such items are prevalent in our society.

The best way to combat these negative influences is to have your children involved in as many different types of positive activities as possible. There are many out there. Use your imagination. Filling the vacuum in your children's lives will increase the odds of positive outcomes. Idleness tends to lend itself to depression and mischief.

One more note. Although the Internet has much good and is now needed for many homework assignments, never leave your children unsupervised on the Internet for long periods of time. Do not allow them unlimited access. Many dangerous things, from pornography to sexual predators, are easily found there and will play to your child's natural curiosities and weaknesses. Use security software and/or parental settings, and remain alert!

Personal cell phones also provide many new challenges because of easily accessible social media applications, such as Snapchat. Be vigilant.

16

Morning Routine

Many children in care take medications. To be certified as a caregiver, you will most likely attend trainings on this.

In short, many children in care are depressed and take antidepressant medications. Many have been diagnosed with attention deficit disorders and are given medications for that.

Many medication directions will say, for instance, "Take one pill in the morning." Our routine for many years was to wake the children in the morning; let them get dressed, do their chores, and eat breakfast; and then give them the medication they needed.

Getting teenagers moving in the mornings often requires waking them up more than once and constant vigilance. We often had to make several trips to the different children's bedrooms to make sure they were up and about. Children with attention deficit disorder have a hard time focusing and staying on task; therefore, it often took a long time for them to get dressed and clean their rooms. We considered this normal.

After many years we had a brainstorm, the result of which has saved us labor and time. We changed our morning routine! Now when we wake up the children, they all come to the kitchen to receive their medication first. This way we know all are out of bed. That saves time. The children then eat breakfast and then get dressed and clean their rooms. The way this helps us most is that medications for ADD work fairly quickly. They enter and leave the systems much sooner than some other medications. By giving the children their medication first, we allow time for it to get into their bodies before they begin their chores, etc. It is unbelievable how much that simple routine change has helped us.

17

Professionalism

Therapeutic childcare is a profession, just as being a minister or teacher is a profession. It should be a respected profession because of its importance rather than denigrated because of the negative image some of us create. I have a friend who supervised many foster homes. He once told me of a set of parents who received a new child in their home. The following day they sent the child to school on the bus with a note that said, "Please enroll me in school." I don't believe that this is the type of reputation we need. Anyone can do better than that. Here are some things we do and things that are important.

Dress professionally. By that, I mean dress appropriately for whatever you are doing. If you are at the movies, you might be in casual attire. At church, you should probably dress up somewhat. If you are going to the school or a doctor's office, dress appropriately. I have seen parents in this profession wearing pajamas to talk to the school principal. I personally don't want to be associated with that. Try to remember always that we are setting an example for our children.

My wife does most of the school contacts in our family due to work schedules, although I also do at times. Our good relationships with the teachers and principals have made it much easier for our kids to transition into the school system. We try to make ourselves readily available to faculty if needed. They have all our telephone numbers, including our cell numbers, where they can reach us anytime with a question or problem. One of us can usually be up to the school within fifteen minutes if needed. Make sure you attend all meetings with teachers and others when they're regarding your child. Try to make weekly contacts with teachers. Internet access makes this easier, but make sure to also be seen personally often. We try to attend as many extracurricular activities as possible, because this helps our children feel that they belong to something and that we are supportive of them. Try to always attend open house at the schools, art exhibits, and other functions.

To be professional, you must remember that confidentiality is a must. In fact, it is required by law that some things regarding a child's history remain confidential. Curious friends ask us many questions about children's pasts. We explain to them that we can't discuss it, and most people respect us for this.

If someone calls you requesting to talk to you, then call them back or meet with them.

To be professional, just act professional. There will always be someone watching and formulating an opinion of you, even if it is just your own children. Make sure the opinion they formulate is positive. Others' positive opinions can open many doors to you when you are in need and help your overall situation in other ways as well.

18

Listen to Reports from Others

Situations with troubled children are almost never as they seem. When my wife and I first got into childcare, we must have been the most naive and gullible pair to ever set foot in a group home. If you can get out of a phone booth without written instructions on the door, you are probably smarter than we were.

We believed everything our kids told us and nothing other people said. If we had a negative report concerning one of the children in our care, we would ask the child about it. The child would promptly deny it, and we would decide that everyone else must be wrong. This child would never lie to us!

Our first hard reality check concerning this occurred soon after we began our career. We received reports from parents in another home that an older boy we had in our home was sneaking out at night and visiting a girl on campus regularly. The parents in the other home had never caught him, but some of the girls had informed them. We immediately questioned him, and of course, the girls in the other home were, according to him, just trying to get him in trouble. My wife and I were beginning to suspect we weren't as vigilant as we'd thought. The male parent from the other home and I devised a trap. We placed pennies on the edge of the boy's window against the screen one night. The next morning, we checked. We wouldn't have had to bother with the pennies. We wouldn't have needed them. On close examination, I discovered that the window's screen was attached upside down. We went into the bedroom to look, and an empty bed was underneath the window. It was an unused bed and was made up at all times. In the middle of the pillow of the freshly made bed was a perfect imprint of a size twelve shoe pointing away from the window. It looked like an exhibit from a court television show. We learned at that particular time, to our dismay, that some kids are very, very good liars.

We learned after this to always issue consequences to a child after what we considered to be a reliable negative report. It didn't matter how profusely the child denied the incident. Consequences were issued.

This was done for some good reasons. If the child were guilty, then it was just. If the child were not guilty, we would eventually find out. The child would be mad, of course, but he or she was learning to accept consequences appropriately, even if those consequences were not fair at the time. Eventually everyone has to suffer consequences unfairly, and enduring this is a skill that everyone needs to function properly in society. It is a lesson best learned earlier in life than later, when it can cost a job or relationship. When we sometimes found out later that we had been wrong, we would apologize and give rewards. The child could come out of this situation having learned something either way.

Remember, you are not a caregiver or a parent trying to win popularity. You are trying to raise kids who can function in society.

Also, don't beat yourself up if your children outsmart you from time to time. It happens to everyone. Just learn, and go on. The kids are depending on you.

19

Be Open to Criticism

Always be open to constructive criticism and training. Developing this willingness and openness is hard for most people. This is a skill we expect our children to learn and possess, but our human nature often makes us unwilling to accept feedback from others in a positive manner. Anyone with any amount of experience can usually benefit from an outside observation coming from a trained and caring observer. Remember the old adage, "You can't see the forest for the trees." Sometimes what we need to help us in a situation is obvious to someone distant and uninvolved but impossible to find when we are close to the issue ourselves. Never dismiss someone else's opinion or advice before careful, unemotional deliberation. You will never grow if you are unable to learn this. In sports, you would be referred to as "uncoachable."

20

Make Memories

The children placed in your care will often have a very limited view of the world. They will probably have never seen or experienced what we take for granted. We live in central Texas. It is 350 miles to the Gulf of Mexico, but most children we get have never seen the ocean. They cannot even imagine it.

We once asked one of our children, while planning a vacation, if she had ever been to the ocean. The child said yes, and my wife asked her where. She replied, "The one in Lubbock." If you aren't from Texas, find Lubbock on the map, and you will understand.

We feel it is important to take your children on a vacation each year. Try as much as possible to show them new things and let them have new experiences. Most summers we will take a trip to the coast, because as I said, most haven't seen the beach. They love it. We go to theme parks, state parks, fairs, rodeos, movies, ball games, concerts, and anything else we can. It does cost money but you can budget for it. The memories the children make will last a lifetime.

Your entire experience with the children in your home shouldn't be about confronting negative behaviors. It is just as important to learn to have fun as a family. Children need to know it is possible to have fun without drugs or alcohol. Travel and family fun broaden their perspective of the world.

Every type of pleasurable experience doesn't have to cost a lot of money. Children often enjoy simple things as much as expensive things. Take a visit to the local park. Visit the movie theater. Looking at Christmas lights is always a big favorite. A barbeque with homemade ice cream is something most have never experienced. Holidays at home with a big, happy family are great. Both my wife's family and mine dine at our home during the holidays.

I once came home and found my wife and the girls baking sugar cookies for the holidays. When they were done, she gave about half a dozen to each of them and then brought out a tray of sprinkles and icing. Each child decorated her own cookies however they wanted. Some were spectacular. While all of this was going on, I asked my wife what they were doing, and she replied, "Making memories." My wife can be great fun. I have also seen them decorate Easter eggs, which can be great fun too.

Remember that when things are going well and the kids are having fun, you should enjoy the experience yourself. Often helping others to have fun is the most fun of all.

We have a girls' home now. Most girls have never had a positive male role model in their lives. One thing I try to do on Valentine's Day is to give each girl a long-stemmed rose or carnation. At the same time, I bring roses home to my wife. It makes them feel special for a while, and for many it is the first time they have ever received a flower from anyone.

As I have gotten older, I have realized I like to give things to others rather than receive. I like that feeling.

Christmas is a tough time of year for most of our kids. Everything around them, from school to advertisements on television, makes them sad because they are not at home with their "real" families. My wife works very hard at getting gifts and cooking. Our older biological children and their families all come to our home at the holidays because it is the only place we can all fit. Although the children in your care may not be able to spend holidays with their biological families, it is important to make them feel that they fit into yours. Many children have told us how much they appreciated this. It can make you feel great too!

21

Learning from Disagreement

It is natural to have an argument with your spouse. If you think it should never happen, then you're from Mars. No two people can agree on everything. Human nature takes over, and an argument ensues. The longer I have been married, the more I have learned to give up quicker, but that is another story.

If you have an argument with your spouse that ends without physical aggression, name-calling, or someone leaving, then the children in your care learn a valuable lesson: all arguments don't have to end badly.

It is okay for parents to disagree occasionally; in fact, it is normal. The main thing the children learn is that after an argument, two people can still care for each other without anything bad having occurred. Most of the children in your care have a completely opposite remembrance from their biological homes. You have just modeled a better example. Giving your spouse a little kiss later doesn't hurt either.

The children also learn how to disagree appropriately. This is an important skill that we all need to be successful.

22

Keeping Your Sanity

To survive as caregivers, you and your spouse must have a similar value system and similar sense of morality. This is often the rock you will have to fall back on when you feel that everything has failed and you are at a loss as to what to do. If you and your spouse are not in agreement on basic moral or value-based issues, you will most likely have many disagreements. I have seen many marriages fail due to this when coupled with the stress of being caregivers to emotionally disturbed children.

I honestly do not know how single parents survive as caregivers. There are many out there, and my hat is off to them. I believe it takes a person of unimaginable strength to survive in this situation alone.

Learn your spouse's strengths and weaknesses, and truthfully evaluate your own. In our home I believe my strongest asset is my ability to remain calm and on an even keel during stressful situations. I know I am not the most dynamic person in our family. That would be my wife. She has the ability to instill excitement and fun into everyday life. She can come up with many fun experiences for the kids and has the ability to share the emotional highs and lows. They will confide in her easily. The downside to that is that it can be very draining emotionally and there are times when she needs to be alone to recharge. This is where I come in. It works for us, but everyone's relationships and their experiences will be different. The point I am trying to make is that to work with your wife day in and day out, you must be able to "switch-hit," as they say in baseball. You may each have your normal routines and habits, but you must be able to switch roles with your spouse when needed, and sometimes you must be able to do it all. Everyone gets sick, tired, or discouraged. It is at those times that the other spouse must shoulder the load and readily step in. This is essential to survive and to successfully help the children in your care.

In the childcare profession, *respite* is a term that basically means "time away from the children in your care." My wife and I have found it vital to get away from everyone for a day or two at least once a month. Giving to and caring for an emotionally disturbed child is an endeavor that can be stressful, tiring, and draining on both physical and emotional levels. Take time each day for some quiet time if possible.

Finding someone to take care of the children in your care while you are away is often difficult. Each agency will usually have its own ideas and strategies. Use all options available to you. It is important for your emotional wellbeing and personal happiness that you keep your batteries charged, and sometimes this can only be done by taking a break. I remember one point, when we had not had respite for several months, I went as far as to rent a motel room in our hometown so that my wife and our younger biological children could get away for a couple of nights. It was well worth the expense. My wife told me it was the nicest thing I had ever done for her.

Remember, even God rested on the seventh day.

23

Sharing Disciplinary Duties

What I am about to share is important. If you and your spouse cannot learn this skill, it will be difficult to be successful.

You and your spouse must be equal partners as much as possible when it comes to unpleasant chores, such as disciplining or confronting a child over negative behavior. Do not fall into the trap of letting one parent do all of these types of interactions. At the same time, if one parent is confronting a negative issue, he or she must see it through to the end. If the other parent jumps in and takes over, trouble will follow.

It is normal in most non-foster families for one parent to do the majority of the heavy discipline. Most of us can still remember hearing our mother tell us, "Just wait until your father comes home!" When raising emotionally disturbed children, this is unacceptable, and I will explain why.

Children in care will often test the limits in their home and of their caregivers. It is a constant process. If one caregiver always issues the negative consequences or often has to come to the aid of the other caregiver, then the children will soon perceive the other caregiver as weak. When the weaker caregiver is alone with the children, abnormal acting out will occur. It will become very difficult for this caregiver to maintain order. Children must feel safe, or they will act out in many different ways. When one child begins to test the limits of the weaker caregiver, another child may begin to feel unsafe, which will cause that child to act out also. This has a snowball effect until eventually the weaker caregiver is unable to manage the children alone.

Children must feel safe and that someone of strength and resolve is looking after them at all times. They must feel that the caregiver they are with can handle any situation. If this is not the case, disorder and chaos often follow.

24

Don't Be a Child's Peer

Never try to be the best friend of a child in your care. In the childcare profession, this is called *peering*. This may sound quite the opposite of what you believe, but it is important.

Children do not need more friends or a new best friend. They have friends. What they need most is a parent. Parenting is often not much fun, but it is important, and it is your job. You job is to set and enforce limits, reinforce values, praise the positive, and hold your child accountable for his or her actions. If you spend most of your time trying to be a good friend to the child, your real job as a parent will become impossible due to conflict of interest. I have often told a child, "Sometimes being a parent is a cruddy job, but someone has to do it, and right now that's me, whether I like it or not."

25

Sexual Acting Out

Many children in care are promiscuous or will become so if left to their own devices. Watch for this, and teach to it. Take appropriate precautions, and supervise your children's opposite-sex relationships as much as possible. Know where your child is at all times. This will often help prevent some unwanted opportunities from becoming available.

If you have several children in your home, always try to notice subtle things. Some children are by circumstances natural victims. Occasionally some children are by nature and prior circumstances capable of perpetrating sexual abuse on other children. This will most often happen in a home with a mix of older children and younger children. Most often I have found it to be in all-male homes, but it can happen in a home with any mix of children.

Most caregivers will never know abuse is taking place. The victims or perpetrators will never admit to it. Watch for the younger children acting out behaviorally in a sexual manner, or sometimes they will just act out more often than normal. A perpetrator will often give his or her victims gifts or special treatment. It could be candy, toys, favorite games, money, or any conceivable item. Sometimes just being favored by the perpetrator, if the perpetrator is older, will be enough. Watch for an older and younger peer spending a lot of time together. Because of these possibilities, we have learned to have certain rules in our home that help prevent or make it difficult for this to occur.

We do not let a child in our care buy candy or items for just one particular peer unless the child has our permission and it is for a special occasion, such as a birthday.

We never let children with a large age difference share a bedroom.

Children are not allowed in each other's bedrooms unless they have our consent each time.

Children are never to close their bedroom door unless they are changing clothes, and then they must be alone.

More than one child is never allowed in a bathroom at the same time.

Never allow secrets in your home. Most abusive homes have many secrets. If one child does something wrong and another child knows about it and doesn't tell us, then both have consequences. The children will argue that it isn't fair and that they don't like to tattle on people. Ignore this argument. Deliver consequences to both. The children will soon learn your expectations and comply.

Secrets are the main source of power that manipulators and perpetrators use. They will agree to keep secrets, such as a peer's misbehaviors and transgressions, to themselves. Later, they will threaten that peer with exposure if the peer doesn't give into the perpetrator's demands. Children are often illogical in their thinking, so threats like these will often work. Children must learn not to keep secrets if they are to develop the skills needed to protect themselves from abuse.

We try to enforce these rules consistently and without failure. Everyone in our home knows this, and it often helps prevent serious or dangerous events.

It would be very hard to forgive yourself if a child in your care were abused because of your ignorance or carelessness.

Be watchful. Many children in care are capable of unspeakable acts due to the abuse and training they received in their biological homes.

Make sure abuses stop at your doorstep. Be vigilant.

26

Avoiding Sexual Allegations

If you are a foster parent or caregiver, you must be aware of your situation regarding the children in your care and the possibility of sexual allegations being made against you. It can happen.

Many children in care have been sexually abused, and many are known to lie on occasion. If a child is upset with you, this can be a bad combination. We have been able to avoid these situations by staying vigilant and following specific rules and policies we have in our home.

At present we operate a home for girls, so I will speak from the male perspective in this, but it can be transferred to opposite situations and different homes.

I will never go into a girl's bedroom alone unless the door is left completely open. We have a rule in our home that all doors must be left cracked open unless someone is changing clothes.

I never take a girl anywhere alone in a vehicle or remain alone in the home with her unless she has lived with us for a very long time and has earned trust with us. Remember, just because a child has lived with you for a long time does not always mean the child can be trusted. In the transportation of a child, this sometimes poses a problem. If you must transport a child who is new to your home, then I recommend you do as I do and always carry a witness. It can be another child who you trust; I have often used my biological children. In the past I can remember hiring my daughter to ride with me on trips to the airport.

If I feel a girl is dressed too scantily, I send her to change into something more modest immediately, and by the same token I make sure that male members of my household wear shirts and are dressed appropriately as well.

Many girls in care have been sexually active in the past. Many have also learned to manipulate older men using sex. Be watchful for this type of child, because there are many out there, and they always test a male parent figure. This type of thing now also happens with a male child and a female foster parent. Always be watchful, and plan ahead.

Finally, if you have taught and earned the trust of the children in your care as you should, they will most often be protective of you and help keep you out of trouble. They will often know of another child's plan or tendencies long before you have realized them yourself.

Be very cautious!

27

Keeping Your Biological Family Together

When we became parents in a group home, we brought our biological children with us, of course. Keeping a balance and knowing what to do with the relationship between our biological children and the children in our care was uncharted territory, and I have heard very little training or advice on this issue to this day. Most parents, I have found, pay little care to this, and dire consequences sometimes follow.

What my wife and I know on the subject we learned from our experiences, and we have fortunately been able to avoid most pitfalls by learning from the misfortunes of others.

When a child moves into your home, you may or may not be aware that the child could possibly return to his or her biological parents at some time. Most children will do so after care, even if their abuse was severe. This is a sad reality. Keep this in mind, and combine it with common sense when mixing your biological family with others. We all want to make a new child feel like he or she is at home, but the reality is that most children will have two families—yours and the one they will return to.

If you treat your biological children exactly the same as the children you are now caring for, you may find that in the end you have lost your children while trying to care for someone else's. If you treat the children in your care unfairly, then resentment and problems will arise. There is a fine line to walk.

Here is what we have done and what we do. We explain to all children who come into our care that our biological children are housed separately. By this, I mean they have their own separate bedroom close to my wife and me. Also, my wife and I will sometimes vacation separately with our biological children. Some of the children in your care will resent this, but we explain by telling them that we help other children because that was a choice that my wife and I made. It was not a choice that my children made. I also explain that they have their own biological families and that in time they may want to reunite with them. We explain that it would be cruel of us to abandon our own children in order to help others. They are usually satisfied with that answer.

You must salvage your biological family's unity and meet your biological children's needs, or you will fail. I have seen it many times. My wife and I spend special time alone and quality time with our children away from everyone else. When they were young, we also often involved our children in a particular sport or activity that only they participated in. When the children in our care went to bed, we would often sit and talk with our biological children or watch a special television show with them. We always take a trip or vacation as a biological family unit. Make your biological children feel special and loved, and show them that you are available. If you can do this, your children will be fine.

While you want to make your biological children feel special, you must make sure you do not treat them as such when both sets of children are interacting. When our children were young, we always expected them to adhere to the same rules as everyone else. At no time did we allow our biological children to be elevated during normal interactions. We always tried to hold our biological children accountable and at the same time teach them to have caring and generous spirits. We always dined together and attended normal events, such as church, together. All of us went on vacation together and attended normal family activities as a larger family unit. When you are careful, fair, and have a caring spirit, God will allow you to balance this fine line without hurting anyone.

Some children in your care will try to use your children as leverage to get special favors from you. They will often do special things for your biological children and go out of their way to befriend them. If successful, they feel they can then get special favors from you. We were never 100 percent able to prevent this, but in most instances we were.

Never allow the children in your care a lot of unsupervised time with your biological children. Monitor what is going on at all times. There are many children in care who act out sexually and are even sexual predators. Don't be fooled into thinking your child will always be safe because you trust a certain child in your care. Even the wisest of parents can be fooled. I have seen several parents and their children devastated over a few incidents of lack of supervision and misplaced trust. Consequences can run from rape to unwanted pregnancy. I have seen it all. My wife and I vowed not to ever make this type of mistake and to learn from others. I hope and pray that you listen to my words and save yourself and your family from almost certain heartbreak. Be ever vigilant! A little careless supervision can lead to permanent heartbreak.

28

Working with Families

When a child is placed into your home, it is important to understand that it may be for an indeterminate length of time. Some children may be in your care for years and others only a few days. Many different things out of your control determine this.

All children will have individual stories, but many aspects of their histories may be similar. After learning their story, you may feel mixed emotions from pity and sadness to anger and outrage. I try to remember the old adage "But for the grace of God go I" and thank God for my childhood and home. The goal of the childcare system and the courts is to try to reunite families as often as possible if the reason for the child's removal from the home can be corrected. Many parents are basically good people who do love their children but have made mistakes due to negligence or difficult circumstances. The parents themselves have often been dealt an unfair hand and have difficult obstacles to overcome. If these issues concerning the child's welfare can be resolved through counseling, therapy, or training, then it is in the child's best interest to return home. If this cannot be done, sometimes grandparents or other relatives may come forward and care for the child. Those who do should be commended. It is a sad statement about our society that so many have neglected and abandoned their children to the care of other family members or the welfare system because of misplaced priorities.

In most instances, the court system will give parents every opportunity and a lot of time to correct their problems unless the problem involved criminal actions. In these instances, the child will usually not return home unless a suitable relative is available.

A child will not be eligible for adoption by anyone until the case has worked itself through the court system and the parent's rights have been terminated or relinquished. This procedure may take years or never happen at all. Both are common.

As a caregiver, you will often be required to contact or supervise contacts between the children in your home and their biological families. This could be by telephone, letter, or visitation. Many times it may be inconvenient, or you may feel it is not in the child's best interest. You must remember that the decision is not yours and is often court ordered. Try to be upbeat and positive about these familial contacts. Be professional and courteous at all times. Most children will look forward to the visits with excitement and anticipation. Some children may act quite the opposite and be hesitant and apprehensive. Be ready for both possibilities.

Many children in care may be available for adoption at some point in their care, but the fact is that few will be. The children in our care come with baggage, and it takes a caring and dedicated person to adopt one of them. If you feel this is your calling, then I both applaud and encourage you.

We have had many children in our care who have had parents serving prison sentences connected with their abuse. At first glance one would believe the children would demonstrate anger toward the parents, but that is most often not the case. I have often seen the children harbor feelings of guilt because they feel it is their fault that their parents are incarcerated. They will almost without exception be in denial about their abuse. Many will make excuses for their parent's actions, defend their parents, write them often, and talk about their plans to reunite when their parents get out of prison. The parents usually seem to be in the same state of denial and tend to blame others for their crimes.

It takes a very long time to heal a child after severe abuses have occurred. I have found that in severe cases, very few ever recover completely.

Even though a child's parents have made mistakes, you must support the child in his or her reluctance to abandon his or her biological family. That is sometimes a tall order but important.

Just as importantly, you must sometimes do the unpleasant task of preparing a child for the possible failure on the part of the biological parents to do what is required to complete the reunification process as required by the welfare system or court. This often occurs for the same reason the family split in the first place. Some parents will just not put forth the effort. The child has a hard time understanding, and you are required to pick up the pieces.

Be prepared for a child to act out behaviorally after visits with his or her biological families. Any type of behavior can occur. This is because of all the emotions connected to the visit, and the child will often have a hard time transitioning from the lack of structure in his or her family unit to the more structured environment you have in your home. After a few visits, the negative behaviors will usually come less frequently. Hang in there, and expect them. These behaviors are normal.

Many older children will experience alcohol, drugs, and other negative influences on home visits. You can expect that also. If you find this out, just notify your supervisor about the incident.

It takes a lot of patience and understanding to work with children during these tough situations. If your heart is in the right place, you will learn over time how to handle most of these. It takes experience and cannot be easily taught.

Don't wear your feelings on your sleeve, because there are many opportunities to get hurt.

29

Cultural Awareness

The distance between the life I lead and the life my father has led is as far as London is from Tokyo. My father was responsible for very little inside the home as far as chores were concerned. I remember several years ago, when my mother went out of town for a couple of weeks, she left written instructions on the washing machine so he might wash his clothes in case of an emergency. I admire his ingenuity in pulling that off for a lifetime. In my life I have learned on occasion to cook for twenty to thirty people at mealtimes and to conduct all aspects of domestic maintenance as needed. I learned none of this from my childhood.

I have lived with children of different races, ages, and origins. This is also a big difference. Many caregivers will most likely have a very diverse mixture of children as far as race and origin goes. To be successful, you will need to work with these different children and adapt to their needs. I remember a time when the only children in our home of the same race as my wife and me were our own children. Many years ago, at six years of age, my daughter learned to dance exactly like MC Hammer, who was popular at that time. She had a lot of very talented teachers in our home.

It is important to not harbor any prejudices, because you will be found out by your actions. This line of work is not for someone with deep resentments. All children must be treated fairly and equally for you to be effective in raising a positive child. If a child sees that you have prejudices, you will be unable to be a successful teacher.

Prejudices from within will not be the only obstacle to overcome. Be prepared for some children and their biological families to harbor deep-seated prejudices and fears of you because of *your* race. You must learn to dismiss them as best as possible and refuse to harbor resentment. Fairness from you will help to overcome most of these issues over time.

My wife and I have come to realize that it is important to celebrate other cultures and heritages as much as possible. We don't feel as caregivers that we should force children of other cultures to adopt our lives exactly—only our morals and values. We try to celebrate holidays and traditions important to others as much as our own. Black heritage celebrations, Martin Luther King Jr. celebrations, and Cinco de Mayo celebrations are good examples. It is important that children who are allowed to visit their biological families be able to attend family reunions and other family events. On vacations to Corpus Christi, some of the girls like to have their pictures taken beside the Selena memorial. My wife has learned to do hair extensions like a professional. Because, as mentioned earlier, many children will return to their original homes after their time in care is finished, it is important for them to remember where they came from. Lead with your heart, and most everything else will fall into place.

On a personal note, I believe my biological children have benefited from their experiences growing up in a diverse home. I believe they truly are colorblind, and in fact, we have probably integrated and educated segments of an entire community from our home.

30

Splitting

Many children have learned how to manipulate others extremely well, and their skills are impressive. They can often manipulate their caregivers as well as their peers. It is common for a child to "split a couple," or play one adult against another.

If you find yourself arguing with your spouse often concerning issues involving a particular child, then you can be sure that child is working his or her magic on you. Team up with your spouse to find out how the child is causing the split.

Don't be embarrassed or upset if this happens to you. It has happened to the best without having been found out until later. Often couples never find out what was causing the stress in their homes.

The child who is causing this problem for you will most often be the child you find easiest to talk or interact with. The most charming children are many times the ones who give you the most trouble. It's just that you don't know what is happening.

31

Learning to Let Go

I have learned much about letting go. My wife and I joke that after we got into the childcare business, we learned to let go of the expectation of having friends invite us to their homes on Saturday nights. We also learned to let go of expectations that friends would visit us often. That is the reality of what we do. Our busy lifestyle takes most people out of their comfort zones.

As a foster parent, I have learned there are many things to learn to let go of in order to secure your psychological well-being.

You must learn to let go of negative feelings after negative encounters with a child. You must learn to start fresh every day.

You must learn to let go of hurt feelings on a daily basis, because you will have your feelings hurt often. It is the nature of our profession as foster parents.

Learn to let go of a child when he or she leaves after graduation or is emancipated from your care. We have probably cared for several hundred children in our careers. All were special, and all had special places in our lives.

Learn to let go when a child leaves to go back home. These children are not ours. We only keep them for a short time. Because this time is limited, make the most of it.

Learn to let go of a child when you do not have the experience or knowledge to help him or her. You will never be able to fix everyone's problems, no matter how hard you try. You must learn to accept this and let some of these children go where someone else could possibly give them what they need. Let's suppose you were visiting your family doctor regularly for checkups and he discovered that you had a rare illness. Your doctor would, of course, send you to a specialist or another doctor with more extensive training and experience in caring for your illness. It wouldn't mean that he had given up on you. It would only mean that he was doing what was best for you because he knew he didn't have the needed skills. He would be negligent or remiss if he did anything less. If you are not succeeding in helping a particular child, you need to realize that you may possibly not have the skills needed to help that child. You will need to let go and help the child transition into a placement that might be more effective. You have not failed. You have done what is right for the child. No one can be everything to every child. Every childcare provider needs to learn his or her limitations. When it is in the child's best interest, let go.

I have a variation of an old prayer that I sometimes think of when I feel I have failed a child: "Lord, give me the strength and knowledge to help those I can and the wisdom to know whom I cannot help."

You can't save all children. Do what you can. Take comfort in the fact that you did what you could and kept them safe while in your care.

32

Exaggerated Illness

Most children who come into care were neglected when they were very young, which will often manifest as exaggerated symptoms when the children experience minor illnesses or injuries. Many children will demand medicine or doctor visits concerning these exaggerated pains or symptoms. Most often these demands are cries for attention. Treat them as such.

Try to treat all injuries or sicknesses as you would for anyone else. Do not allow panic, exaggeration, or hysteria to ensue. Try to downplay minor incidents as just the normal part of human existence that they are. Over time most children will settle into your home comfortably, and these incidents will usually decrease in frequency. If an injury is serious, then by all means treat it as such, but do not exaggerate your sympathy toward the child.

I just give out Band-Aids and Tylenol sparingly and downplay the minor events.

Do not reward negative behaviors, or they will increase. Be appropriate in your response to the level of crisis.

33

Confrontation, Unpleasant but Important

Most people are non-confrontational by nature. My parents were, and I was raised in that manner. Most people will do almost anything to avoid confronting a child about a negative behavior. Most people do not want to deal with the inevitable backlash, so they avoid it as much as possible. The ability to confront a negative behavior from a child or a problem as such can be taught and learned. The most important thing to remember is that it must remain an unemotional response for it to be successful. A simple example could be that the trashcan is full and needs to be emptied. Try to view confronting a behavior in the same manner. You would not get mad at the trashcan. It's just a thing that must be done, so you take it out. After taking out the trash, the chore is done and forgotten.

Confronting a behavior should be handled in the same manner. It's just a thing, so to speak—an unpleasant task. Do it, and move on. Stay out of the interaction emotionally, or it will escalate! Emotional involvement in the interaction is normal but unproductive. This will require a lot of work to learn if you have a quick temper.

It is very important during a confrontational interaction to use a calm, unemotional tone of voice. If the child's voice is raised, then try to lower yours. In most cases this will help to calm the interaction. Occasionally a louder, firmer tone is needed, but it will take experience to learn when this is more effective; until that time, use it sparingly.

My wife and I learned to confront negative behaviors early in our careers. We were taught a method that confronted all negative behaviors, both large and small, as they occurred. It became almost second nature to us and still is to this day. We also learned by repetition to detach ourselves emotionally from these interactions—much like the taking out the trash example.

If I had to pin down the one thing we do that has allowed us to maintain order in our home over the years and keep our sanity, I would have to say it is our willingness to confront a negative behavioral problem head-on, without hesitation, no matter how inconvenient, and see it through to a favorable conclusion.

I admit that when we started in this profession and began confronting negative behaviors in emotionally disturbed children, we quickly learned a lot. I learned many things that I didn't know about my ancestry, where I should go, and what I should do when I got there. Because of my sheltered life as a child, I was not previously aware of many things and was quite shocked to hear them, even angry.

Confrontational exchanges are much like watching a horror movie for the first time—terrifying and emotional. After you watch the movie many times, however, you can take a nap during it without worry or fear. In fact, you can look at the screen and know what is about to happen next. It isn't scary at all. Over time, confronting a child can become just as unemotional and predictable. It just takes practice and self-control.

When confronting a child over a negative behavior, there is one thing that will help keep things under control but is seldom taught: Remove the child's audience before the confrontation begins. If other children or adults are with you, ask them to leave the room, if possible. In a public environment, try to get the child to follow you to a more private area before you confront the child. I am usually successful by instructing the child to follow me and then turning and walking away. In most instances, the child will follow. When I have isolated the child, I will begin my teaching interaction with him or her. Children's behaviors will usually escalate in front of their peers. If this happens, you will often lose control of the situation. I have seen simple confrontations begin to look like an episode of *The Jerry Springer Show* at worst or at least an interesting episode of *People's Court*.

My wife and I will never allow a child in our presence to disrespect us or others, pick on a peer, exhibit insensitivity or meanness to another, or do anything we feel is antisocial or inappropriate for the situation without addressing it. The children soon learn this about us, and it saves much work. We basically teach what is acceptable and what is not as it occurs. If the behavior is small or unintentional, we will do it privately or possibly later but if it is major or has occurred previously, we confront it at that moment.

When I have to confront a child, the rest of the world has just stopped as far as I am concerned, and it doesn't restart until I am satisfied with the results of my teaching. I do not care how long it takes! My wife is much the same way, and all the children in our care know it. A teaching interaction will last until the child accepts what he or she has been told to my satisfaction and the negative behavior stops. When I say "negative behaviors," I mean all negative behaviors. I expect a reply in a correct tone of voice, or that will have to be corrected also. The child may not always agree with me, but he or she learns to answer appropriately and do as I ask or we continue until he or she does.

I try to never compromise what I believe is appropriate behavior.

As I said, this goes as far as the tone of voice the child uses to talk to me. It will be a pleasant voice without sarcasm, or we will practice that also until I feel it is correct. If I ask a child to sit down at the table, then I expect him or her to calmly walk to the table and sit down quietly. If not, we will practice that until correct. We then move on to the original problem.

Over time I have learned that a child will get just as mad and upset when redirected over a small behavior as when it is a serious matter. Do not ignore small behaviors and save confrontation for only the large issues in an effort to save yourself some trouble. You're not saving yourself any trouble. If you teach to the small things, often the large things will not occur. As a result, your life is simpler.

Have you ever watched a small child who has stepped on a grass bur? Sometimes the child will sit down and cry because it hurts but will not pull it out or let anyone else do it for fear that it will hurt worse. It is inevitable the grass bur will have to be pulled out, but the child will suffer for a long time if this is delayed. When the child does pull it out, it will hurt sharply, but the pain will soon go away.

This example is identical to delaying confrontation with a child over a negative behavior due to fear or dislike of the tantrum that will follow. You may ignore the behavior, but eventually it will escalate until it cannot be ignored and will have to be confronted. Save yourself the lengthy stress and suffering. Confront the child immediately. Deal with it. Get on with your day. After learning this skill, you will find that your stress level will go down and your life will become easier. Just like taking out the trash, confrontation is just a thing. Do it, and move on.

If a person does something long enough, it will become a habit. If it is positive, it will become a good habit. We have found that over time most kids will come to accept what they have been taught as the way things should be. They often begin to think of these teachings as things they learned on their own. Everyone's daily life gets easier and less stressful. The chances of the child being accepted into society later increase dramatically.

This all begins with a willingness to be confrontational in spite of the difficulty or unpleasantness of confrontation.

I once heard a popular comedian talking about disciplining children. He remarked that times had changed since he was a child and that now you are supposed to give children time-outs. He said that the only time his father gave him a time-out was when he took time out of his busy day to spank him. That is also my basic memory of discipline as a child. However, when disciplining a child in foster care, spanking is not tolerated. Other methods must be used due to the abuses some children received before being removed from their biological homes and in order to meet current guidelines and practices.

I use time-outs often when dealing with negative behaviors. A time-out is when you isolate a child away from other people and distractions while giving the child some quiet time to regain composure and self-control. The child should also be thinking about what he or she did wrong and what would have been a more appropriate course of action.

After a child does something inappropriate, I will redirect him or her concerning that issue. If the child begins to argue, make excuses, or respond in any manner other than what I expect, I then will ask him or her to go to a neutral spot I have designated and take a time-out.

I have come to the realization that I can often bore a child into submission much easier than I can by threatening with consequences. Sometimes after asking a child to take a time-out, he or she has responded with, "I don't need one." On occasion I respond with, "Maybe not, but I do. Please go sit down." This goes back to my point about staying unemotional during an interaction.

If you feel yourself getting angry, let the child take a time-out, and use the time-out for yourself to regain your composure.

When a time-out is needed at home, I usually ask the child to take it at the kitchen table, which is most often isolated from the other children. If the child refuses to sit at the table as I expect, then I allow him or her to take this time-out while sitting on the floor in a designated area that I can easily observe.

After what I believe has been an appropriate amount of time, I will discuss the original problem with the child. I expect the child to accept responsibility and express willingness to make a change. If this does not happen, I will let the child sit there longer and ponder the issue. If after our second discussion things are still not resolved, I usually give the child a specific time at which I will come back to discuss the issue. This time period will be longer. Giving the child a specific time that I will return will sometimes help him or her realize how much of the day this tantrum is costing. I usually go into another adjoining room from where I can monitor the child without the child monitoring me. Some children are very stubborn, so this can go on for some time. I have found that all of these situations must end to your satisfaction or you will just have to repeat them again very soon.

Most children soon begin to understand that I am possibly the most stubborn man in the world, even more stubborn than they are. As I said earlier, it is often easier to bore a child into submission than to use threats of consequences. I once sat in my recliner and read a magazine with the weather channel on mute and a child beside me in a time-out for what seemed a very long time. This child never gave me another problem. If that isn't legalized torture for a child, then I don't know what is.

If you are going to try to maintain order in your home with emotionally disturbed children, then you need to study their behaviors. Learn their likes and dislikes. Believe me: they are studying you. This is important, because you need to use logical and natural consequences for negative behaviors. You need to know your children and be able to adapt consequences to fit each child for this to be effective.

If you have a child who is a loner and depressed, grounding him or her is worse than useless. Being alone in his or her room is what the child wanted all along. A better consequence might be to prohibit the child from spending time in his or her room or force the child to spend time in the family room with another grounded peer.

If a child is very social and enjoys noise and interactions with others, then grounding this child to the dining room to read might be more effective. If a child will not go to bed on time or is reading after lights out, I will normally have the child sit in the kitchen and watch me read. The child will soon be begging to do what he or she wouldn't earlier. Another consequence might be to get everyone up earlier in the mornings until the behavior changes. Most children hate to get up early.

If a child will not clean his or her room properly or pick up his or her possessions, then I may do it for the child. The catch is that I keep everything that I pick up in another room until I feel the child can keep his or her room straight by him or herself.

If I go to pick a child up from school and the child makes me wait needlessly while he or she socializes, then I may be intentionally late the next day so that it is inconvenient for them.

You are probably seeing a pattern here.

Some caregivers use work as punishment, but I don't. I feel this teaches children to hate work at a time when they need to learn it is a privilege and a necessity.

I have been to many college classes and extra training sessions that teach the secrets to modifying behavior. I have come to the realization that there was never a secret at all. The only thing you need to do is make it more convenient for a child to do what you ask than not.

If you are consistent with this and you are as stubborn about it as my wife and I are, then the children will learn that it is much easier to do what you ask. As I said earlier, these learned habits will usually begin to transfer to other areas of their lives. If this happens, then you have succeeded in producing a more socially adaptive and productive person.

34

Power Struggles

When you have reached a stone wall with a child concerning something you want the child to do, arguing or threatening more consequences often will not work.

I have a strategy that I learned quite by accident, and it works most of the time when used properly. I find it to be almost 100 percent effective with lower-functioning or younger children.

What I do is just change the subject to multiple, non-threatening types of conversation. Most kids, when they are mad—especially lower-functioning children—can stay mad about a certain issue for a very long time, yet they are incapable of focusing on multiple subjects at the same time. I will give you an example. Let's just say you have a child named Ann who is refusing to take out the trash. No amount of coaxing, reasoning, or delivering consequences will change her mind. She is intent on defying you. This situation could last for hours. What I might do is ask her again if she is ready to take out the trash. I would hear her give a prompt no. Immediately after that, I might give a moment of silence without a response and look as if I am pondering something. Out of the blue I might say, "I sure did like that movie we watched yesterday; I'll bet you did too." I don't ask for a response. I wait a little bit and then say, "Hey, don't you have a basketball game tomorrow? I heard you might get to play. Could I come?" Ann would probably say, "I guess so." She is then thinking about basketball and not the trash. There would be a long silence. I might then say, "Man, I sure wish we could get this trash taken out so I could go ask Tricia [my wife] if I can go." Another long silence would occur. I would then say, "Hey, Ann, I'll help you with the trash. Let's go get it done." Without looking at her, I would head for the trashcan. More than likely, she would get up and follow me without saying a word. It would have been too much information for her to process at one time, so she would have forgotten about being mad. I would then go with her to take out the trash. I would have gotten what I needed without really dealing with her behavior; but by that time, she wouldn't be mad anymore. When we got back, I would probably turn to her and say, "I sure wish you would have taken out the trash the first time I asked. Since you didn't, you can't watch television tonight; but hey, I'll bet you'll do it next time, and we won't have to be mad at each other again. Okay?" She might say okay without knowing what had happened. The problem might not come up again. If it did, it would usually begin to occur less frequently.

If a child does what you ask enough times, it will become a habit. It is not important what type of teaching you use, just that it occurs.

35

Physical Restraint

The term "physical restraint" is used in the childcare field to describe physically detaining or controlling a child.

The techniques and criteria used will vary depending on what state or agency you live in or work for. All childcare workers, to my knowledge, must be trained in this area and must take continuing education every year.

A restraint is generally used to protect the child or someone else from being harmed or put in danger or to protect valuable property. Generally these are the only instances that are appropriate for using physical restraint. The law enforcement community has a much broader set of reasons they can use to justify a restraint, but as childcare workers, we can't. Mechanical restraints are unlawful unless used in a hospital-type environment or in instances of law enforcement.

The normal person would ask why you would even do this, so I will try my best to explain. Most people have had the experience of watching small children's behaviors. Small children will often throw a fit, as it is called, because they are not getting what they want. Most parents have had to restrain their child at times because of this. An example might be if a child wasn't allowed candy at the checkout line of the store. The child might begin to scream, knock things over, and perhaps lie down in the floor where he or she could be in danger of hitting him or herself on something, being stepped on, or experiencing some other danger. A good parent would most likely pick up the child and carry the child to safety or hold the child tightly so that he or she could not get free until able to control him or herself. Another example could be a child who runs out into a busy street. A good parent would immediately pick up the child, carry the child to safety, and remain holding the child until the child could remain safe.

These types of behaviors will sometimes be seen in childcare with children much older. The children were not disciplined or taught when they were younger. They will continue to throw tantrums at these older ages because in the past they would usually get their way. Most likely their early caregivers were unwilling or unable to put forth the effort to correct the behaviors or deal with the embarrassment.

An older child who exhibits these tantrums and outbursts is more dangerous and their reactions are more severe than those seen in a smaller child.

This being the case, physical restraint is often the only method available and effective in protecting the child until the child is under control. As a caregiver, you will sometimes be forced to act. Anything less would be negligence. This action is often a shock to both the child and the caregiver. You just hope that soon the child will learn a more appropriate response to anger. Children usually begin to understand that dangerous actions will not be allowed. I have found that performing a physical restraint is always very unpleasant but sometimes necessary. A restraint and the reasons for use are almost always completely misunderstood by the general public. I have found that most new foster parents and even many experienced parents misunderstand its uses and effects.

Try to avoid performing a physical restraint in public if at all possible. Make sure it is the only way possible to keep a child safe.

Many times the general public will feel a child is being abused and will call local law enforcement if they witness a restraint, however justified.

The child being restrained is mad and will play the attention received for all it is worth. You and your agency may become vilified in the public eye. It does not matter in most cases that the restraint was justified. You will appear in a negative light to all witnesses. In public, raise your tolerances a little, and use restraint only if it is certain that severe harm will occur if you fail to act.

Early in our careers, a close friend was forced to perform a physical restraint on a child in public because of suicidal actions. This restraint was completely justified, needed, and performed properly. Because it was in a public place, an investigation with much second-guessing and speculation occurred. He and his wife's careers were almost ruined, and they considered leaving the profession. In the end they were vindicated, but the stress and scrutiny they had to endure was horrific. They both remained in the childcare business and have helped many children since that time. We learned a valuable lesson from their experience. I hope you will have the wisdom to learn their experience as well.

I believe that using a physical restraint could be compared to a country going to war. It should be done sparingly and only as a last resort, but all should know that the resolve is there if needed.

Your home will run smoothly only if all children feel safe. Occasionally a child will be placed into your home that has unsafe outbursts. The child will often push boundaries until they break and safety becomes an issue. For all to be safe and feel safe in your home, everyone must know that you are capable and willing to restrain a child if the situation warrants it. They must know that it will be quick once the decision has been made. Eventually, most caregivers will be tested. You will receive the training you need from your agency, so don't worry about that at this time.

My wife and I seldom need to perform a physical restraint. A child that needs to be restrained often is likely inappropriate for foster care and may need to be placed in a more restrictive environment with clinical staffing.

A common mistake made by caregivers is to become emotional during a heated altercation with a child. Becoming emotional can sometimes lead to a restraint that might have otherwise been avoided if the caregiver had remained more focused. Many caregivers feel that restraining a child will punish the child and that somehow this will force the child to comply more easily. This thinking often leads to unjustified restraints and unwanted outcomes. Granted, the child was out of control and the caregiver frustrated, but a different way can usually be found.

Restraints can be dangerous even when performed correctly. Caregivers and children alike can be injured and many times are. If you perform a restraint properly, the child will be uninjured. You will most likely wake up the next morning stiff and sore with bruises, while the child will be completely unharmed.

I have never restrained a child without wishing another solution could have been found.

As I said, restraints are dangerous and to be avoided if possible. Children have been killed during restraints. That would be hard to live with.

Restraints will also cause relationship damage and will take much time to overcome. Not performing a restraint can often teach more than performing a restraint, but it takes experience to learn how to avoid these situations.

In short, children must know that you are capable of doing what is needed to keep everyone safe, but you will also not do anything that is unjustified. With this knowledge, the children will develop a trusting relationship much sooner.

Trusting someone means that you believe the person will do what is right and proper when needed. This is true in both negative and positive situations. If you can earn this type of trust from your children, then the battle is half over.

36

Faith and Worship

I believe it is important to have a religious faith, but do not push your foster children into your faith. Just teach them and be a role model. As the child attaches to you and you develop a relationship, the child will, in most instances, attach to your faith over time. This will occur if you are consistent with what you believe and not hypocritical in your actions.

You need to also know that if you don't have a faith, most likely the child in your care will not develop a faith either. I believe that a faith in God and, most importantly, a relationship with Jesus Christ will help us when nothing else on earth can.

My observations over the years have shown me that most children are desperate to believe in something. Most are looking for a quick fix to their pain and loneliness. Many will convert to whatever faith you show them very quickly. It is our duty as caregivers to teach that it takes time, effort, and work to develop a lasting faith. It is never a quick fix. It also follows that since our children have a vacuum in their lives and are searching for solutions, they will adopt negative solutions just as quickly. If you don't have a positive example for them, they will usually find an answer you didn't expect and didn't want.

Youth groups at churches are an excellent resource. Kids can be introduced to faith while interacting with other youth in a fun, positive environment.

Lead and teach by example.

37

Conclusion

As I get older, I understand better that everyone has flaws. Some are just not readily apparent. Often during our marriage, my wife and I have remarked on how much we admired what a good marriage some people seemed to have. A few years later some would be divorced; when we heard the news, we were stunned. They were good people; we just didn't see everything.

I don't feel that only people who appear perfect make good foster parents. Good foster parents are common people with good judgment and morals who feel led by something within or by circumstance.

Many young boys want to play in the National Football League, but few opportunities exist to become a superstar. In life, the opposite is true. Few people want to be or feel they can be successful foster parents, but many are needed. This is a place where you could easily become a superstar in a younger person's eyes.

During our years of raising other people's children, we have experienced both success and failure. We have had children become the first in their family to graduate from high school or college. We have had children get married, have children of their own, and become productive members of society. We have also had children leave to go back to filth, poverty, and abuse, but it was their choice to make. We do not get to choose for others. All we get to do is show them our lives for a short period of time and care for them. The choices that we make personally can often have a profound effect on others long after the fact. Which child is taken into your care, which agency you are affiliated with, or which church you attend are good examples of this. Our family switched church bodies at one time for reasons that we did not fully understand. Later, foster children we had not even met at that time and were later placed in our care were led to Christ. Sometimes our simple actions can be multiplied mathematically to help others we do not know or may never meet. Be sensitive to the Spirit.

When I regret a poor choice a child in our care has made after leaving our home, I think back to when we first started our careers. A supervisor we had early on had much experience. He told me of a married couple that was dear to him and his wife. It seems the couple had been in the foster care profession for a number of years. After caring for a young man for a good part of his life, they adopted him. The young man left home for college, where he committed a terrible crime. The couple was devastated, as you might think. They questioned themselves, God, and their entire life's work. In time, they came to realize a truth that they shared with my friend: Our job in this profession is to do the only thing we can do, which is to keep the child safe while in our care. That then allows the child the opportunity to make choices later in life, whether right or wrong. Without us, the child may have never had the opportunity to choose. We are here to keep the children safe.

As I said earlier, we struggle every day. We struggle for us, and we struggle for those entrusted to us. I still don't know how we do what we do, but I know who has provided for us. We don't see him or always seek him, but he is there just the same, every day. We do it with God's help.

Tommy Storey

The Christian who is pure and without fault, from God the Father's point of view, is the one who takes care of orphans and widows; and who remains true to the Lord—not spoiled or dirtied by his contacts with the world.

—James 1:27 (The Living Bible)

Manufactured by Amazon.ca
Acheson, AB